Monster Jokes

COMPILED BY PAM ROSENBERG • ILLUSTRATED BY BOB OSTROM

The Child's World

Special thanks to Katie Cottrell for her
assistance in compiling source materials.

Published by The Child's World®
1980 Lookout Drive • Mankato, MN 56003-1705
800-599-READ • www.childsworld.com

Acknowledgments
The Child's World®: Mary Berendes, Publishing Director
The Design Lab: Design
Jody Jensen Shaffer: Editing

ISBN 9781623239985
LCCN 2013947278

Printed in the United States of America
Mankato, MN
November, 2014
PA02251

5

VAMPIRES

What's a vampire's favorite holiday? Fangsgiving Day.

Why doesn't the vampire have a lot of friends? Because he's a pain in the neck.

What's a vampire's favorite fruit? A neck-tarine.

What dogs are the best pets for vampires? Bloodhounds.

How would a vampire like to see a horse race finish? Neck and neck.

What would you get if you crossed Count Dracula and Jesse James? A robbery at the blood bank.

How does a vampire like his food served? In bite-size pieces.

Why was the young vampire a failure? Because he fainted at the sight of blood.

What is Dracula's favorite landmark? The Vampire State Building.

What's a vampire's favorite sport? Batminton.

Why aren't vampires welcome at the blood bank? Because they only want to make withdrawals.

How do you join the Dracula fan club? You send in your name, address, and blood type.

What's the difference between a baseball player and a vampire? One bats flies and the other flies bats.

SKELETONS

What happened to the ship that sank in the sea filled with piranhas?
It came back with a skeleton crew.

Why didn't the skeleton dance at the party?

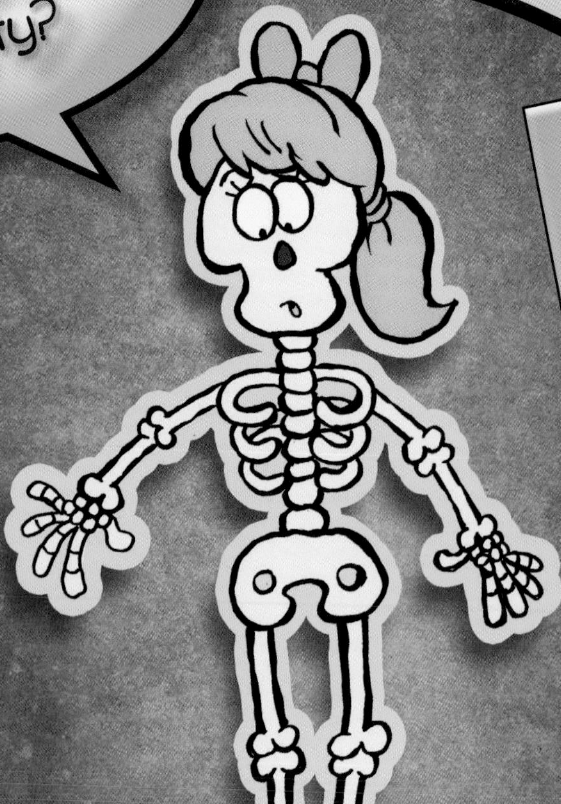

Why don't skeletons play football?
Because they can't make body contact.

She had no body to dance with.

Why did the skeleton laugh? Something tickled his funny bone.

What do you call a skeleton who won't get up in the morning? Lazy bones.

Who won the skeleton beauty contest? No body.

What kind of plate does a skeleton eat off of? Bone china.

Why don't skeletons play music in church? They have no organs.

What does a skeleton order at a restaurant? Spare ribs.

Who was the most famous French skeleton? Napoléon Bone-apart.

WITCHES

Why do witches ride on broomsticks? Because vacuum cleaners are too heavy.

What do witches put in their hair? Scare spray.

What is a witch's favorite subject in school? Spelling.

Why don't angry witches ride their broomsticks? They're afraid they'll fly off the handle.

What do you call a witch's garage? A broom closet.

How do witches travel when they don't have a broom? They witch-hike.

Why did the witch keep turning into Mickey Mouse? She kept having Disney spells.

What do baby witches play with? Deady bears.

What noise does a witch's breakfast cereal make? Snap, cackle, pop!

What happens when you see twin witches? It's not easy to tell which witch is which!

Who flies on a broom and carries a medicine bag? A witch doctor.

What do you get if you cross a witch and an iceberg? A cold spell.

What do you get if you cross a dinosaur and a witch? Tyrannosaurus hex.

MONSTER TONGUE TWISTERS

Peggy Babcock's mummy,
Peggy Babcock's mummy,
Peggy Babcock's mummy.

Mummies munch much mush;
Monsters munch much mush;
Many mummies and monsters
Must munch much mush.

If two witches watched two watches,
which witch would watch which watch?

The wretched witch watched a walrus washing.
Did the wretched witch watch a walrus washing?
If the wretched witch watched a walrus washing,
where's the washing walrus the wretched witch watched?

GHOSTS AND GHOULS

What kind of street does a ghost like best?

What position did the monster play on the hockey team? Ghoulie.

Why did the ghost go to the carnival? It wanted to go on the rollerghoster.

DEAD END

A dead end.

What do ghosts eat for dinner? Ghoulash.

Why are graveyards so noisy? Because of all the coffins.

What airline do ghouls fly? British Scareways.

Where do ghosts get an education? High sghouls.

What kind of music do ghosts dance to? Soul music.

Where do ghosts go on vacation? Lake Eerie.

What trees do ghouls like best? Ceme-trees.

What did the baby ghost eat for lunch? A boo-loney sandwich.

MISCELLANEOUS MONSTER JOKES

What's a monster's favorite soup?
Scream of tomato.

What happens if you upset a cannibal?
You get into hot water!

What inning is it when the Frankenstein monster is up to bat?
The fright-inning.

Where do zombies go on vacation?
Club Dead.

What do black cats eat for breakfast?
Mice krispies.

What do you call a hairy beast that's lost?
A where-wolf.

What did the cannibal order when he went to a restaurant?

A waiter.

Why was the werewolf arrested at the butcher shop?
He was caught chop lifting.

What couldn't the coach of the zombie team say to his players?
Look alive!

Knock knock.
Who's there?
Zombies.
Zombies who?
Zombies make honey, and zombies don't.

GIRL MONSTER: Mommy, my teacher said I was neat, pretty, and well-behaved. MOMMY MONSTER: Don't worry, dear, you'll do better next time!

Knock knock.
Who's there?
Voodoo.
Voodoo who?
Voodoo you think you are?

What does a cannibal call a skateboarder? Meals on wheels.

What happened at the cannibals' wedding party? They toasted the bride and groom.

How can you help a starving cannibal? Give him a hand.

What did the cannibal say when he was full? I couldn't eat another mortal!

About Bob Ostrom:

Bob Ostrom has been illustrating children's books for nearly twenty years. A graduate of the New England School of Art & Design at Suffolk University, Bob has worked for such companies as Disney, Nickelodeon, and Cartoon Network. He lives in North Carolina with his wife, Melissa, and three children, Will, Charlie, and Mae.

About Pam Rosenberg:

Pam Rosenberg is a former junior high school teacher and corporate trainer. She currently works as a author, editor, and the mother of Sarah and Jake. She took on this project as a service to all her fellow parents of young children. At least now their kids will have lots of jokes to choose from when looking for the one they will tell their parents over and over and over again!